CONFIDENCE

How To Boost Your Self-Confidence and Self-Esteem, Turn Your Life Around And Be Confident In Any Situation.

ZACHARY D. WEST

Introduction

I want to thank you and congratulate you for buying the book, *"Confidence: How to Boost Your Self-Confidence and Self-Esteem, Turn Your Life Around and Be Confident in any Situation."*

This book contains proven steps and strategies on how to improve your confidence by correcting how your mind works – to make it work in your favor.

Low self-esteem is a disease of the mind. It is not real, more often than not, but it stays inside of you and creates a lot of damages to your entire personality. It affects your present and your future.

This book will teach you to solve the problem from the root—your own mind. It explains where the problem comes from and why it continues to get worse. Furthermore, you will be presented with easy-to-apply strategies to improve your mental, emotional, and physical states.

Thanks again for buying this book, I hope you enjoy it!

Chapter 1: The Different Levels of Self-Esteem

When you see a girl with an unusually long neck, what could be the first thing that comes to your mind? Would the word "freak" pop out first? Do you tend to laugh right at the first glance?

Most people would give intriguing glimpses followed by grins or laughter simply because their concept of beauty does not match that of the girl with a long neck. In fact, that kind of physical appearance would be "freakishly" unusual in many cultures.

However, do you know that among the women of the Kayan tribe of Burma, wearing stiff neck rings to elongate their neck and drop their ribs signifies strength and beauty? They deliberately wear neck rings and add new ones as they grow up because their standard of beauty is different from yours. The same is true for the women of Africa's South Ndebele tribe where wearing neck rings signifies social status and wealth.

Classifying standards

Go back to your reaction upon the sight of the girl. What could have been your reaction? What could have made you react that way? If you laughed or raised an eyebrow, would it have been instinct or conscious decision? How about pity? Would you have felt sorry for the girl?

Most people would be curious, while a few would not care at all. Those with aroused curiosity would stop at just being curious. Others would proceed to judge while the rest would resort to ridiculing the girl. A last group of people would feel pity for the girl.

From the example above, you can easily determine each person's level of appreciation and standard of beauty just by seeing their reaction.

- Those who do not care about the girl's appearance have unconditional appreciation.

- Those who are merely curious have conditional appreciation. They weigh things according to norms and values, with the tendency to give the benefit of the doubt. They can hate and they can love, but they need a compelling and valid reason to lean towards one side.

- Those who judge right away have discriminating standards. They already have a definition of what is good and bad, and what is acceptable and unacceptable. They will not even change their views based on the circumstances involved. They either see the girl as attractive or unattractive. No ifs, and or buts'.

- Those who laugh at or ridicule the girl have either a superiority complex or narcissistic tendencies. Many of them ridicule others to show superiority, but the truth is that they are hiding their true feelings of inferiority and insecurity. Some of them simply love themselves too much — so much so that they feel above everyone else in every aspect, and that they are without any flaws. They might laugh with or without the malicious intention to offend and ridicule. That is because their discriminating standards are usually subconscious, although they do show up in their actions.

- Those who feel pity for the girl have an inferiority complex. They show empathy towards the girl because they think that they would also pity themselves if they were in the girl's place.

A discriminating standard implies that there is a distinct line separating the positive perception from the negative perception. It develops into an instinct eventually, which is even more harmful to your self-esteem. At this point, you have to decide to which group you belong. It is not too late to change your attitude and mindset. Just believe that you are capable of changing for the better.

Healthy confidence vs. overconfidence and lack of confidence

From the five groups of people with different standards, only the first two groups have healthy levels of self-esteem. They do not judge themselves unless they have to. They focus on their weaknesses as much as they do on their strengths. They accept the fact that they have weaknesses that they can improve, and that they have strengths that they need to continue honing. They acknowledge that they can be either right or wrong, depending on the circumstances involved.

On the other hand, the last three groups have unhealthy level of self-esteem. They either ooze with overconfidence or lack confidence altogether.

Having too much self-esteem is bad because it makes a person too blind to see his or her own mistakes and flaws. In the process, they fail to identify the areas that he could have improved. Their pride is stopping them from taking action, so their bad qualities get worse, while their good qualities remain dormant. People who display too much self-esteem tend to believe that they are superior, possibly blinding them to realizing they lack far behind most people.

Similarly, having poor self-esteem makes a person blind to see his or her own good qualities. People with poor self-esteem feel inferior because they only see their flaws. They do not believe the compliments and faith given to them by other people because they are too busy doubting themselves and wallowing in self-pity.

It is essential that you develop a healthy level of self-esteem; this will allow you to accept your flaws and listen to and integrate constructive criticism without losing faith in yourself.

Zachary D. West

Chapter 2: **Changing Your Negative Mindsets**

Picture two neighboring families; both have small boys, but they lead very different lives.

The first child lives in a family consumed by bigotry and conceit. His parents always call him ugly and tell him he will never amount to anything. His parents first establish his standard of acceptance, and this standard is being continuously reinforced everyday through comparisons, insults, maltreatments, and physical abuse.

The second child lives in a family bonded by love for each other, accepting who they are and loving their own qualities, believing that they are gifts from the heavens. His standards of acceptance are not grounded in prejudice, but on the acceptance and trust of the people around him. These standards are reinforced every day with compliments and encouragements that do not discourage or sacrifice honesty.

As the first child grows up, he becomes unaware of the other possible standards of acceptance. He shuts himself off from the opinions and appreciations of other people, as they were unfamiliar to him. Even after he leaves his home, he still has in his mind the standards that he's learned, adopting them as the ultimate truth through time. They become his mindset, and become difficult to change over time once strongly engrained in the child's mind.

On the other hand, the second child grows up understanding that he is not perfect, but that he is capable of improving his physical, financial, spiritual and relational attributes, abilities and demeanors. Because his parents taught him, when he was still a child that humans come in all shapes and colors, he knows that every person has his or her unique qualities.

From the example above, the second child will go on to become more emotionally flexible than the first. He will favor the positive in people and situations though he will most likely not dismiss the negative right away. After all, he knows that he is not perfect himself either.

He is aware that he may not be where he intends to eventually be in life, but he accepts this fact because he knows that he can change this through hard work. He knows that his abilities are far from perfect, but he is still proud of his abilities nonetheless because they can be improved with continuous practice and dedication. He understands to weigh his core strengths more heavily than his core weaknesses. His concept of possibilities allow him to explore new dimensions of his personality, not limited by a permanent line that separates the good and bad, the beautiful and the ugly.

And you may wonder - why is it so hard to change mindsets even after identifying them? It is because they are already inculcated in your core just like your values that have been built and reinforced through time.

Attitudes that are reinforced from childhood onwards are the strongest and most persistent. They were imparted at a time when the mind was still at its most vulnerable. As Bill Clinton writes in his autobiography My Life – there is nothing more powerful to develop an attitude of love and understanding than a childhood surrounded by people who make you feel that you are the most important person in the world.

This being said, you may be at a stage in your life where you feel that it might be difficult to change your attitude and mindset. But fear not - it is never too late to change your mind. Everyone can become more confident at any point in time.

Before you continue reading, prepare to have an open mind and look at yourself objectively. There is a good chance that you fall in one or all of the categories below, because next, we will look at some of the most common symptoms of low self-esteem.

1. Chronic indecision

Serious and repetitive indecisiveness that affects your ability to function is called chronic indecision. Generally, a person with a big decision to make will weigh all aspects and details, pros and cons, benefits and consequences before taking a final action or giving a final opinion. That is being cautious and analytic.

However, if your inability to decide affects your normal daily life—from choosing the color of the shirt you are about to wear, to choosing which dish you are going to cook—there is a possibility that you may have a self-esteem problem.

Decisiveness is the result of self-confidence in making the right decisions and assessing situations. It indicates that you are comfortable with your own abilities, knowledge and intuition - enough to take a risk despite not knowing with certainty the outcome of your decision. This level of confidence gives you courage to pursue your goals and accept as well as reflect on your mistakes. Hence, one of the most effective ways to improve your self-esteem and boost your self-confidence is to continue making decisions, with or without assurance. In the words of the famous self-help guru Tony Robbins, "the best way to make better decisions is to make more of them".

But why is it that some people experience chronic indecisiveness in the first place? It is because they fear the uncertainty of the outcome. They fear making mistakes; they are afraid to realize they may not be qualified enough to make an important decision; they fear what other people are going to say about them. It is no wonder that Napoleon Hill, author of "Think and Grow Rich", states as the sixth limiting fear of mankind, the fear of criticism.

Making big decisions is hard, no doubt about it. But if you refuse to take risks, you will never learn. Learning to make decisions is just like trying to learn how to ride a bike; you fear the possibility of falling down and hurting yourself, potentially being ridiculed by others around you, but you still push through because there is no other way to learn it.

Do not look at your decisions as opportunities for other people to make fun of you and question your abilities. Everybody makes mistakes once in a while – including the most powerful leaders from all imaginable walks of life. Even the ones who will ridicule you have made wrong decisions, without the shadow of a doubt. Never be ashamed of yourself for making mistakes because you are not the first and definitely, will not be the last. To paraphrase Tony Robbins again, fail forward! Learn from your mistakes, and move forward. Remember that good judgment is the result of experience, and experience is often the result of bad judgment.

Here are some action steps you can take to get yourself moving forward, in the direction of more confidence and self-esteem:

a. *Always give it your best shot.* Your best might be good enough. If it isn't – at least you tried! There are times when the effort is more valuable than the outcome, and there are many times when the outcome is still appreciated even if it is not what is wanted. Most people will not dismiss the hard work that you put into something, especially by the ones with unconditional appreciation.

Accept the fact that you can never get all decisions right; that there are many factors that can affect the outcome of every decision. Sometimes, even the right decisions can end up wrong when the circumstances are just not right.

"Remember that you never want to fail because you didn't want to work hard enough. Leave no stone unturned".
- *Arnold Schwarzenegger*

b. *Take calculated risks.* More often than not, the most successful businessmen are not 100% sure of their decisions. Even Bill Gates had mild successes with some of his ventures (ever heard about Microsoft's tablets and hybrid computers?). Donald Trump ended up in bankruptcy once. Even Martha Stewart, who was broke in 2004 after decades of financial success, bounced back higher in 2012 to become one of the richest entertainers in history once again.

All of them made wrong decisions—major ones. But what kept them successful is their courage to take calculated risks. They made decisions with no guarantees, but with big possibilities of success.

No divine entity can give you the right decision. You have to work hard for it by learning as much as you can.

c. *Learn from your mistakes.* Do not be ashamed of your mistakes, but be ashamed of yourself when you do not learn anything from them. Multi-billionaire and hedge fund manager Ray Dalio sees "an incredible beauty to mistakes, because embedded in each is a puzzle, and a gem that could be obtained if solved – i.e. a principle that could be used to reduce mistakes in the future". You can never waste anything in making a decision. You get it right, and you earn the reward. You get it wrong, and you learn a lesson. It is up to you if you will use that opportunity or not.

2. Envy

A disproportionate feeling of envy is another common symptom of low self-esteem. Remember - admiration is different from envy. A person who admires someone becomes inspired and motivated to improve, achieve more, and work harder without forgetting their own limitations and capabilities.

For example, Marie admires Liza for her exquisite fashion taste. Because of that, she is motivated to work harder to buy the clothes that will also make her look more appealing and fashionably relevant. There is positive motivation.

On the other hand, a person who envies another is impressed, but feels resentment for the realization that someone is better than they are or has something much better than them. Oftentimes, the feeling comes with malice and desire for someone to meet misfortune to lessen their differences.

For instance, Liza envies Marie for having a sexier body. Instead of pushing herself harder to work out and achieve the body of her dreams, she just wishes that Marie would binge eat or become too busy to exercise. It is also possible that Liza would find motivation to work out, but not because she wants to fulfill her goal of becoming sexier, but because she simply wants to outdo Marie.

From the two examples, you can see that both have the same objective, which is to improve and become better, but with different means. Although the second approach may get Liza fitter in the end, it damages her self-esteem in the process – and possibly her relationship with Marie if the feelings are put on the table.

Envying or admiring?

Ask yourself how you feel when somebody you look up to meets misfortune. Do you feel relieved? Do you feel happy? Do you still feel threatened? These are signs of enviousness that, although malicious in nature, do not always come with bad intentions.

Some people enjoy it when their toughest competitor at work or school does something wrong. They do not actually wish for something bad, but they still feel relieved due to the fact that they will benefit from that mistake. This is the first stage of envy.

Damaging self-esteem with envy

As you lose track of reality, you also start to want bigger things—things that might not be within your reach no matter what you do. Some examples are wanting to grow taller in your 30s; wanting to look like Mila Kunis or Chris Hemsworth; and wanting to wear Prada everyday despite your $20,000 annual salary.

Your frustrations and disappointments become bigger and unmanageable. In the end, your envy will make you feel defeated.

Envy also prompts people to make unnecessary comparisons all the time. There is nothing wrong with making comparisons because it is one way to identify your areas of improvement. What might be wrong is your intention in comparing.

Comparison can be harmful to your mental and emotional state if you do this to justify your decision to stop improving (i.e. I don't have to get fitter because my friends are fatter anyway).

It is also harmful when you compare to justify your reluctance or refusal of a challenge (i.e. Why should I lead the project if I can just sit down and relax at the sideline like the others?).

The truth is that, although admiration and envy are two different things, the line that separates them from one another is just acceptance. Admiring someone means accepting the difference while envying someone means seeing and emphasizing the difference. It does not help to hold resentment against another person because your ill will cannot change your own shortcomings.

Chapter 3: Boosting Your Self-Confidence

Every day, the media shapes your mind without you realizing it. Media, through pop culture and advertisements, slowly, but progressively inculcates concepts of good and bad, of beauty and ugliness, and of right and wrong that may or may not be true in real life. In fact, many of the truths peddled to audiences like you (and I!) are conceptualized and finalized inside boardrooms as part of different marketing propagandas. Unfortunately, the greater influence of media can easily refute other concepts of truths as mere make-beliefs and wishful thinking.

The advertisements of beauty products and fashion brands show what beauty should look like—how smooth and fair the skin should be, how shiny the hair should be, how small the waistline should be, etc. In reality though, beauty can never be standardized because the different cultures and personal preferences that define the standards of beauty will never be all the same. What looks ugly to you might look beautiful to others, and vice versa.

It is noteworthy to mention how many people tend to strongly dislike their very own qualities because of their own insecurities. What you may not know is that other people might also hate themselves for not having the good qualities that you have. Hence, it can be easy for us to get stuck in an endless cycle of insecurity that constantly hurts our self-esteem and confidence for no reason at all.

Stop wandering and wondering, and just stay still for once. Focus on yourself and the things that you have. Look at yourself and not at other people. What do you see? What qualities do you have? How can you make them special? Why should you feel special?

It is about you and not about other people. The following tips can help you realize that and improve what you have.

1. Do not lose sight of what is real

Makeup can enhance beauty and conceal flaws, but what is hiding under the cosmetics still makes up what is real. The consistency, shade, and ingredients can only cover what is underneath, but they do not change your skin.

Making your self-esteem dependent on the material things that only cover your body can be damaging in the long run. Eventually, it makes you believe that your true value is only measured by the things that you wear and own.

Boosting your confidence by looking your best is healthy. In fact, it is highly recommended as it makes you feel special and attractive. It helps nullify the negative feelings brought around by insecurity. However, it is one thing to enhance your innate qualities with material things, and it is another to rely exclusively on material things to feel confident about yourself. Do not let yourself be trapped in a circle of confidence determined only by the mask behind which you chose to hide yourself.

You need to appreciate the benefits of material things to your life, and simultaneously, you need to understand their limitations. Instead of wondering how material things can make you become a better person, think about how you can give justice to the wonderful material things that you wear and own. In a way, it is about *you* making the things you wear look better than they really are, and not the things making you look better than you really are.

2. Admire people for their special qualities, not for their perfection

Admiring perfection only makes you feel imperfect, which is another excuse to lose your confidence. Most people feel insecure because of their ideas of perfection. They constantly look for something that they do not have, and will never have, simply because perfection does not exist. It can never exist because people will always have varying opinions and different standards.

Advertisements transform endorsers into gods and goddesses, but even these high-paying models have flaws in real life. Naomi Campbell earns a million dollars every time she walks the catwalk, but did you ever know that she was already balding? The hottest Hollywood stars always get on the list of the sexiest men and women alive, but they look very different when they don't have makeup on.

The media is giving you a construed reality with perfection everywhere. In effect, you also want to achieve a certain level of perfection, only to be disappointed because that will never happen. It is totally normal to admire people for their special qualities because as aforementioned, people improve themselves by looking for inspirations and influences. The goal is not to have what other people have, but to know what aspects of your personality and body to improve on.

3. Accept that you are bound to be different in some ways

Nutritionists and fitness trainers might see a person with a tall, skinny body as a walking health problem that is just waiting to happen. However, fashion designers and runway coaches might see that same person as a walking million-dollar billboard.

Good qualities are a matter of opinion. Feeling insecure and ashamed of yourself just because some people cannot appreciate you is absurd because those people are just a tiny part of the population. How about the other people who see your good qualities and do not mind your flaws?

Everyone is different from one another in some ways. You should not feel bad about being different because there are billions of people who are in the same situation as yours – virtually, everyone. Instead of hating the difference, celebrate your uniqueness! Your difference can always be an advantage – develop it, and use it in ways that complement your other unique qualities.

4. Look deeper into every negative and positive opinion's real value

If you think that the negative opinions about you are more important than the positive ones, ask yourself what made them more special and believable. Did a disembodied voice tell you about them? Were they written in a magical book excavated underneath the Earth's deepest cave? Were they voted through a national election to reflect the country's consensus? What compelling reason do you have to give more weight to the negative opinions than the positive opinions that you hear?

Negative opinions are no different than positive opinions because they are all just opinions. Believe negative opinions straightaway, and you are bound to feel a lot of negative emotions. Believe positive opinions straightaway, and you are bound to feel a lot of positive emotions. What you are going to believe will affect your emotions, actions, and overall outlook in life.

What to believe is a matter of choice and discretion. Negative opinions can be destructive or constructive. Positive opinions can be fake or real. Automatically leaning towards one kind of opinion will not help you because its real value is hiding underneath. It is not about what kind of opinion you receive, but why you receive that opinion that matters.

If you feel that a negative opinion is constructive and given in good faith, listen to it and learn a lesson. If it is completely baseless and malicious, dismiss it and move on.

If a positive opinion validates your good qualities, efforts, and hard work, learn from the feedback to determine what you should continue doing. If it is baseless and fawning, try to determine and understand the potential malicious intent behind it.

Be critical about everything you hear. Think before you react. Ask before you assume.

5. Listen to yourself before you listen to other people

You cannot respect other people without respecting yourself, the same way you cannot help other people stand if you cannot stand on your own. You have to learn to listen and believe in yourself first before you should consider other people's opinions.

Self-esteem is about what you see and what you hear, or what is shown to you and what is said to you. It is about what you feel about yourself without prejudice to your own unique qualities and capacity to improve. No negative opinion can bring your self-esteem down if you know that there are a lot of positive things about yourself to be proud of. However, you have to acknowledge them first and be your own fan.

Oftentimes, it only takes a good attitude to perk up even if you have noticeable flaws. By allowing your inner self to speak up while you listen carefully, you can find defense for every negative opinion people throw at you. For example, others can say that your fashion statement is awkward and out-of-date, but you can say that you are original and expressive.

Listening to yourself should be about what you want for yourself, and not what other people want for you. You can always consider other people's opinions, but you have to select the ones that can help you love yourself more, not hate yourself more.

You have your own voice for a reason. Use it, and listen.

Zachary D. West

Chapter 4: Embracing Change and Improvement

Change and improvement are necessary to maintain a healthy self-esteem. It is not enough to correct the wrong mindset and learn how to have faith in yourself. You also need to take the necessary action steps to change what you need to change, and improve what can be improved, not because you have to conform to what other people are saying, but because you simply love yourself.

These tips can guide you towards change and improvement without bordering on overconfidence.

1. Create your own style; make your own trend

Supermodels and fashion-forward celebrities show what appeal and attractiveness are all about from their points of view—what signature brands to wear, how to look like a walking catalogue, and what body shape and size to achieve.

However, the people around them also influence the people you admire. Designers dress supermodels, and designers are essentially judged by fashion editors, writers and now, even fashion bloggers. But even they are only judged by their readers, which include you.

The current trendsetters are not pioneers themselves. Lady Gaga has referred to Grace Jones as her influence. Mark Jacobs took inspiration from Grace Kelly's elegant style from the 1950s and 60s. Even supermodel Linda Evangelista once said that she used to mix and match outfits according to what the mannequins wore in the store that she used to pass by as a teenager.

It is absolutely absurd to admire a certain style or trend, and then feel bad about yourself when you fail to copy it. The ones you want to copy have gotten inspiration from someone, or something else. You should do that too and try to create a style that best represents your personality, and not a style that only sells someone else.

Look for inspirations and influences, but do not look for someone to copy inch by inch. It is far better to look nerdy but stand out and feel free, than to look "hot" only to get lost in a crowd of copycats.

2. Keep in mind that the person wears the clothes; the clothes do not wear the person.

Many people have poor self-esteem because they give too much importance to the things that they have and do not have. They do not feel confident in wearing their clothes because their clothes are not the latest designs. They feel insecure at school or work because they cannot wear expensive and signature brands. They are embarrassed to even get close to other people because their jewelries and gadgets are not as flashy as what others have. They come up with different reasons to feel unconfident just because they feel that their clothes are the ones that wear them.

Oftentimes, it only takes swagger to rock a cheap outfit and make it look expensive. Look at how the trendsetter Lady Gaga makes wearing raw meat and police tape look freakish but uniquely fashionable. Look at how former "sexiest man alive" Adam Levine makes worn-out shirts look so sexy. What they wear never defines who they are. They remain special whatever they wear because they always wear anything with confidence and conviction.

3. Improve your existing qualities

There is no denying that looking good and creating positive impressions boost self-esteem. So instead of wallowing on self-pity and questioning the world on why you do not have qualities and things that other people have, why not just get up and actually do something to improve your existing qualities.

First, look at yourself and see the physical aspects that actually need improvement. Can your body get leaner? Can you pack some more muscles or flaunt more curves? Do your skin and hair need more moisture and nourishment? Does your hairstyle complement the shape of your face? Do your clothes complement your height and body shape?

Self-esteem should never be based on appearance, but you need to feel love for yourself by improving what you can improve in your body and style. Isn't that what people do when they care about someone or something? Why can't you do that to yourself? You deserve it!

Second, take a look at your skills and abilities that can still be improved. If you think that you have no skills and abilities to boast, look at the things that you are most passionate about. Passion can lead you to dormant talents and abilities that are just waiting to be discovered and honed. If you really cannot find any, think about your interests. Interest usually comes with knowledge, so find something that you are knowledgeable about.

Hone your skills and abilities by practicing them and actively seeking ways to improve them. You can enroll in classes, workshops, and even read books and watch instructional videos.

If knowledge is what you have, turn that into a field of specialization by learning more from reliable references. Join conversations online with people who share the same interests with you. You can also attend conferences, seminars, and register in online courses and webinars.

Improving your existing qualities can give you more reasons to be proud of yourself, making you feel more confident in the process. Continuously tapping your strengths can also make you feel more confident because you become more familiar and comfortable with your own good qualities.

"Sooner or later, the man who wins is the man who thinks he can."
- *Napoleon Hill*

"He who thinks he can, and he who thinks he can't, are both usually right."
- *Confucius*

Zachary D. West

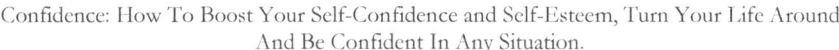

Conclusion

Thank you again for buying this book!

I hope this book was able to help you to build your self-esteem and become more confident in everything that you do.

Learn by heart everything that is written in this book, and ponder how you can continue to improve using this book as guideline. Your journey for a healthier self-esteem does not end with this book. This is just the beginning.

Finally, if you enjoyed this book, then I'd like to ask you for a favor, would you be kind enough to leave a review for this book on Amazon? It'd be greatly appreciated!

Thank you and good luck!

Zachary D. West

Preview Of "Leadership: How to Be a Leader, Boost Your Business Skills and Influence People"

2. Communicating like a leader

Great leaders are excellent communicators. All your ideas will not matter if you do not know how to communicate them effectively to your followers. There are many types of communication that a leader needs to master.

First, you need to develop the ability to talk to a huge crowd. Most people are afraid of talking to large groups of people. If you develop this skill, you will have an advantage over your competition in leadership positions. Here is a process that you can follow on how to talk to big groups:

a.   Identify your objective for talking to the group

Always have an objective when you talk to a group. When you gather people to listen to you, you are using up their valuable time. Without a clearly stated objective, the meeting will have no direction. People may waste time talking about irrelevant topics.

b.   Create a message that accomplishes your objectives

If you are not used to communicating with groups of people, you need to prepare your message in advance so that you can practice it before delivering it to your target audience. This will increase your chances of delivering an authoritative message.

c.   …

Head to Amazon.com to find out more!

Zachary D. West

Check Out My Other Books

Below you'll find some of my other books that are popular on Amazon and Kindle as well. Simply click on the links below to check them out. Alternatively, you can visit my author page on Amazon to see other work done by me.

Wealth: Accumulating Money, Building Wealth and Staying Rich Through Sound Financial Management And Time-Tested Strategies on Amazon.

Leadership: How To Be a Leader, Boost Your Business Skills and Influence People on Amazon.

Positive Thinking: How to Change Your Negative Mindset on Life, Build the Habit of Positive Thoughts and Live a Happy and Successful Life on Amazon.

You can find them on Amazon.com by searching for my author name. Thank you!

www.ingramcontent.com/pod-product-compliance
Lightning Source LLC
Chambersburg PA
CBHW070302190526
45169CB00004B/1506